D0536939

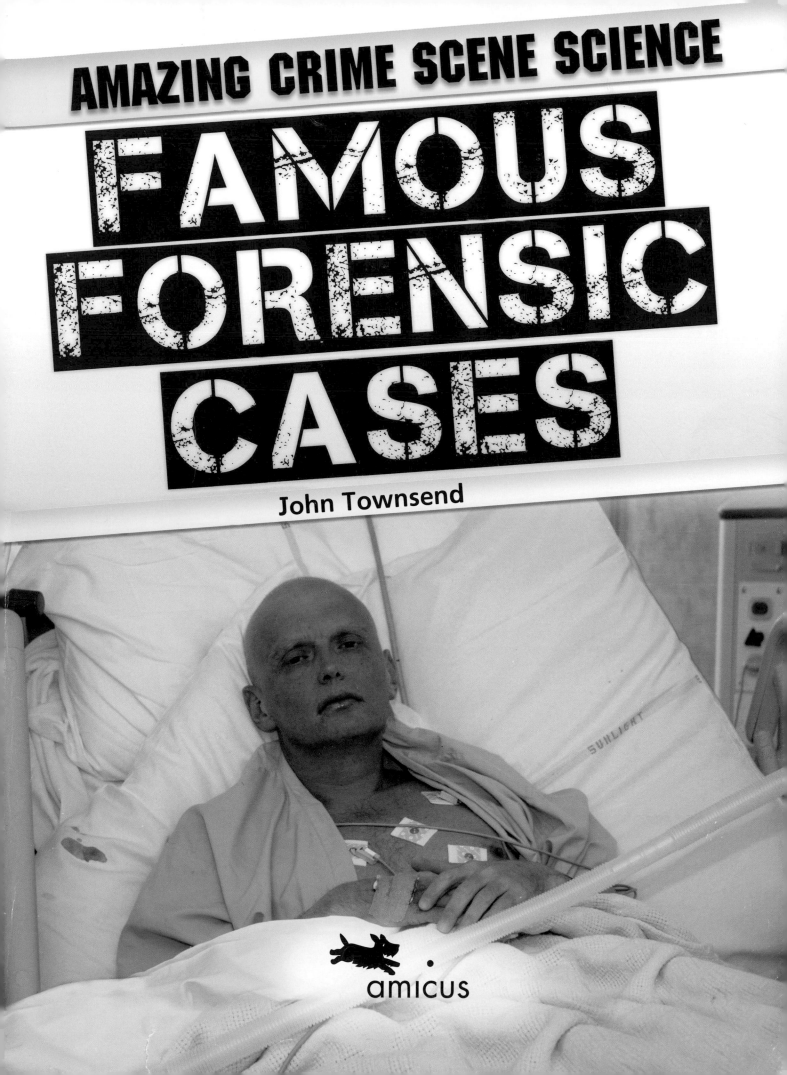

AMAZING CRIME SCENE SCIENCE

FAMOUS FORENSIC CASES

John Townsend

amicus

Published by Amicus
P.O. Box 1329
Mankato, MN 56002

Printed in the United States of America at Corporate Graphics, in North Mankato, Minnesota.

Library of Congress Cataloging-in-Publication Data
Townsend, John, 1955-
 Famous forensic cases / John Townsend.
    p. cm. -- (Amazing crime scene science)
 Includes index.
 Summary: "Traces the cases in recent history that have been solved using the latest forensic science of the time, such as the first case to use fingerprint evidence, hair matching, and DNA profiling. Includes real case files and case studies"--Provided by publisher.
 ISBN 978-1-60753-169-2 (library binding)
 1. Criminal investigation--Case studies--Juvenile literature. 2. Forensic sciences--Case studies--Juvenile literature. I. Title.
 HV8073.8.T683 2012
 363.25--dc22
                        2010044368

Appleseed Editions, Ltd.
Created by Q2AMedia
Editor: Katie Dicker
Art Director: Harleen Mehta
Designer: Gaurav Arora
Picture Researcher: Debabrata Sen

All words in **bold** can be found in the Glossary on pages 30–31.

Picture credits
t= top, b= bottom, l= left, r= right

Natasja Weitsz/Getty Images: Title page, Simon/Shutterstock: Contents page, Anette Linnea Rasmussen/Shutterstock: 4b,
Dusan Po/Shutterstock: 5, Christos Georghiou/Shutterstock: 6tl, Stillfx/Shutterstock: 6tr, Snap/Rex Features: 6b, Hulton Archive/
Getty Images: 7, Hintau Aliaksei/Shutterstock, Dc Slim/Shutterstock: 8bl, Mary Evans Picture Library: 8br, Mary Evans Picture
Library: 9, Andrew Brookes/Corbis: 10, R T Images/Shutterstock: 11, Bettmann/Corbis: 12, Patrick Landmann/
Science Photo Library: 13, Hank Morgan/Science Photo Library: 14, Express Newspapers/Getty Images: 15, Mauro Fermariello/
Science Photo Library: 16, Volker Steger/Science Photo Library: 17, Paul Fleet/Shutterstock: 18t, Jochen Tack/
Photolibrary: 18b, Rex Features: 19, Stephen Alvarez/National Geographic Stock: 20, Natacha Pisarenko/AP Photo: 21,
Zmeel Photography/Shutterstock: 22bl, R. Gino Santa Maria/Shutterstock: 22br, Anke Van Wyk/Shutterstock: 23t,
Sebastian Kaulitzki/Shutterstock: 23b, The Gallery Collection/Corbis: 24, United National Photographers/Rex Features: 25,
Natasja Weitsz/Getty Images: 26, Ekaterina Pokrovsky/Shutterstock: 27t, Jiri Hera/Shutterstock: 28tr, Joppo/Shutterstock: 28cl,
Eric Isselee/Shutterstock: 28cr, Yellowj/Shutterstock: 28bl, University of Glasgow Archive Services, UP1/200/1: 28br,
Dem/Istockphoto: 29tl, Pe Jo/Shutterstock: 29tc, Rex Features: 29tr, Berci/Shutterstock: 29bl, Sebastian Kaulitzki/
Shutterstock: 29bc, Bon D/Shutterstock: 29br, Paul Fleet/Shutterstock: 31.
Cover images: Adam Gault/Photolibrary, Zmeel Photography/Istockphoto, Bettmann/Corbis.

Q2AMedia Art Bank: 4t, 27b.

DAD0052
3-2011

9 8 7 6 5 4 3 2 1

CONTENTS

Early Landmarks 4

Guns and Gangsters 6

Case Study: Famous Kidnapping 8

1950s Science .10

Case Study: 1963 World News. 12

1970s Technology. 14

1980s Crime 16

Groundbreaking Science. 18

Case Study: 1990s Discovery. 20

New Millennium 22

Case Study: Famous Art 24

Case Study: Mystery Poison 26

Forensic Time Line 28

Glossary 30

Index and Web Finder 32

Early Landmarks

Today's amazing crime scene science has a long history of famous **forensic** cases and crime-solving landmarks. Many of these cases helped to develop groundbreaking techniques in detective work.

Early Prints

In 1892, British scientist Francis Galton wrote a book explaining how fingerprints could help to solve crimes. His ideas have been used ever since!

For hundreds of years, scientists have been interested in the particular patterns found on a person's fingertips.

Killer's Thumb

In 1905, two brothers broke into a shop at night in London, UK. The owner heard them and crept downstairs. Alfred and Albert Stratton attacked him and his wife, left them to die, and grabbed money from a cash box.

The brothers were arrested, and Alfred's thumbprint matched a fingerprint on the cash box. Both men went to **court**, where their case made **legal** history. This was the first time a **jury** accepted fingerprint evidence. Both men were hanged for murder.

American History

In 1910, Thomas Jennings robbed a house in Chicago, Illinois, shot the owner, and left four fingerprints in wet paint. Arrested as a **suspect**, his prints matched the paint prints. In court, Jennings was sentenced to death. He was the first person in the United States to be **convicted** of murder on fingerprint evidence.

DID YOU KNOW?

Early fingerprint investigators sorted through thousands of fingerprint records grouped as:

1. Loops: About 60 percent of fingerprints
2. Whorls (spiral patterns): About 30 percent of fingerprints
3. Arches: About 5 percent of fingerprints

Fingerprints were once divided into three main types. Today, a computer can find an exact match in just a few seconds.

LOOP

WHORL

ARCH

Guns and Gangsters

Gang crime was a problem in some U.S. cities during the 1920s and 1930s. Bank robber gangsters sometimes used guns on the streets. To help solve these crimes, the **FBI** turned to fingerprint science.

Machine Gun Kelly

George "Machine Gun" Kelly was a violent armed robber. In 1933, he and his gang kidnapped Charles Urschel, a rich oilman, from Oklahoma City. Kelly demanded $200,000 for his release—the largest kidnapping **ransom** paid at that time.

The St. Valentine's Day Massacre film was made in 1967 about the gangsters who terrorized America in the 1920s and 1930s.

When Urschel was released unharmed, he told the police every detail about where he had been held prisoner. The FBI determined that Urschel had been held at a farm owned by Kelly's father-in-law. The fingerprint evidence at the scene was enough to send Kelly to Alcatraz prison, where he died in 1954.

Robert Phillips

A gangster who knew about fingerprints tried to get rid of his by asking a surgeon to remove the skin from his fingertips and replace it with skin peeled off his chest! Robert Phillips (also known as Roscoe Pitts) wanted smooth skin on his fingertips so he wouldn't leave clear prints at the scene of his crimes. His plan failed, however. When the FBI arrested him in 1941, they identified him from the pattern of ridges on the sides of his fingertips. He was convicted of a burglary after all!

On his 31st birthday in 1934, John Dillinger was declared America's first Public Enemy Number One.

CAN YOU BELIEVE IT?

The famous American gangster John Dillinger (1903–1934) burned away his fingertips with acid to avoid leaving prints behind. He could have saved himself a lot of pain because the skin grew back again, just as before. The FBI killed him in a gunfight soon after his pointless exercise.

Famous Kidnapping

In the 1930s, a big story made the U.S. headlines. It sent a shock wave across the world. The rich and famous Lindbergh family became the victims of a terrible crime.

Missing Baby

In 1932, a kidnapper snatched Charles Lindbergh's 20-month-old son from the family's New Jersey home. The police found a homemade ladder against the baby's bedroom window. The kidnapper had climbed into the room and left a note telling the Lindberghs to pay $50,000 if they wanted their baby back. The Lindberghs paid the ransom money but nothing happened. Two months later, a dead baby was found in nearby woods.

Suspect Found

The FBI traced the ransom money to Bruno Hauptmann, who had more than $14,000 in his garage. Hauptmann said the money belonged to a friend, but handwriting experts matched his writing to the ransom note. Other tests matched the wood in Hauptmann's attic to the homemade ladder at the kidnapping scene, and tool marks on it matched tools in Hauptmann's house. He was convicted of the murder and executed in 1936.

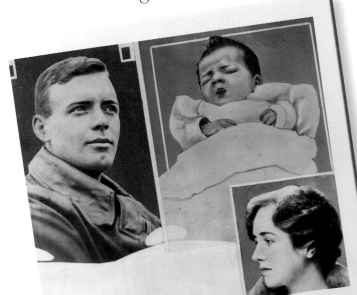

The tragic death of the Lindberghs' baby made headline news in the 1930s.

8

A Real Killer?

This case was famous for many reasons. Mysteries remained and gossip spread. Although the Lindberghs identified the child's body, there was no real proof that the baby was theirs. **DNA** tests were not available at the time, and the body was thought to be too big. Some people even suggested that the Lindberghs' child grew up and Hauptmann had been **innocent** all along. Or maybe the kidnap story was a cover-up to hide a killer in the family. The case of the missing Lindbergh baby is likely to remain one of the big crime stories of the last century.

The Lindberghs were horrified to find a note in their baby's crib.

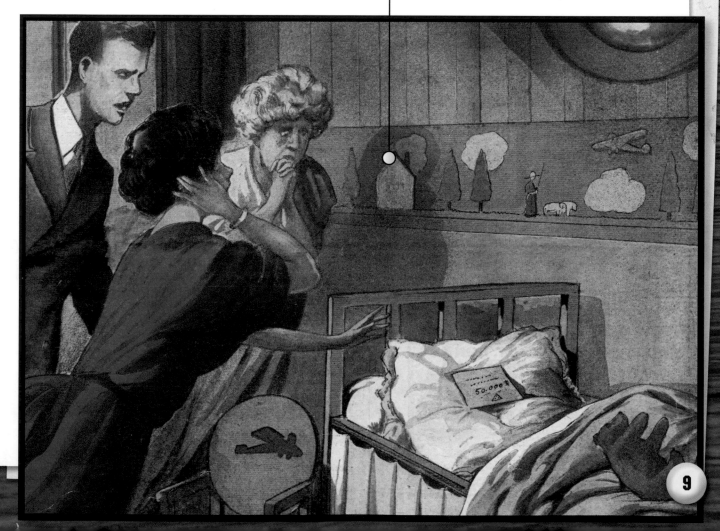

1950s Science

The first crime case to use a special forensic test to match human hairs solved a murder in Canada in 1958. It was groundbreaking crime scene science at the time.

Hair Evidence

One human hair tends to look like any other. At one time, it was impossible to tell the exact origin of a hair found at a crime scene. But things changed. In the 1950s, a new scientific technique called **neutron** activation analysis became an important forensic tool.

When a hair was bombarded with neutrons, its **radiation** could be measured. This helped scientists to test exact details of a single hair and to determine if it came from a particular person.

A human hair can reveal a lot about a person when it is studied in a forensic laboratory.

SCIENCE SECRETS

The latest hair science can show if a single hair is from someone of a particular race and if the hair has been dyed, cut in a certain way, or pulled out. Scientists can even identify the type of diet, drink, drugs, or any poison that the person may have consumed.

CASE FILE

When 16-year-old Gaetane Bouchard from Edmundston, Canada, failed to return from a shopping trip, her father went looking for her. He found her body in a nearby gravel pit with strands of hair in her hand.

When the police spoke to her former boyfriend, John Vollman, who lived across the border in Maine, he denied having seen Gaetane for some time. However, forensic scientists soon proved otherwise:

- Flakes of green paint from a fence where the couple had been seen together recently were matched to Vollman's car.

- A half-eaten bar of chocolate inside the car had Gaetane's lipstick on it.

- A tire track at the gravel pit matched the tires on Vollman's car.

The strands of hair in Gaetane's hand were tested and revealed the most significant identification of her killer. Scientists were able to measure chemicals in the hairs and prove they were from John Vollman. This evidence convinced a jury that Vollman was guilty of murder. He was sent to prison.

Traces of lipstick found on food or cups at a crime scene can be matched to the lipstick worn by a victim or a suspect.

1963 World News

When U.S. President John F. Kennedy was shot by an **assassin**, the whole world was stunned. **Ballistics** experts had their biggest forensic case yet.

Shot in Public

An assassin waited at an upstairs window in Dallas, Texas. He pulled the trigger as President Kennedy rode past with his wife in the back seat of an open-top car in front of a large crowd. Mass panic followed as the dying president was rushed to a hospital, but his life could not be saved. Shock spread around the world.

Big Questions

Despite all the witnesses, photographs, and film footage of the event, the exact details of President Kennedy's assassination raised many questions:

- How many shots were fired?

- How many gunmen were there?

- Where were the shots fired from?

The doctors who examined Kennedy's body were not trained in forensic **pathology** and were unable to analyze the bullet wounds. They could not pinpoint the direction from which the bullets came nor determine how many shots had been fired. They made mistakes when writing their reports, so many mysteries remained.

President Kennedy was in the back seat with his wife, Jackie, when the gunman fired.

Forensic Answers

A ballistics expert called this case a "forensic disaster." He studied evidence and eventually proved that two bullets had hit the president from behind. There was a small hole in the back of President Kennedy's jacket and exit holes through his collar and tie. The other bullet had gone through the back of his head and out the front, hitting a post on the car's windshield. The single gunman, Lee Harvey Oswald, was shot dead by a gunman two days later as the police took him to jail.

This scientist is using a laser to determine the trajectory of a bullet. The laser shows where the murderer may have been standing when the bullet was fired.

DID YOU KNOW?

Today, the science of forensic ballistics is much more advanced than in the 1960s. Bullet **trajectories** can now be calculated with lasers and mapped by a computer to give an accurate reconstruction of a gun crime.

1970s Technology

In the 1970s, new types of **audio** equipment became available and recording techniques improved. This helped forensic experts to measure and match voiceprints from spoken messages.

Voiceprints

A sound **spectrograph** machine turns a voice into a visual display known as a voiceprint. In the 1970s, this technology was used to identify the tone, pitch, and volume of voice recordings.

A forensic scientist uses voiceprints to study audio evidence.

In 1970, Clifford Irving and Richard Suskind claimed that billionaire Howard Hughes had given them permission to write his autobiography. They sold the fake book to a publisher for $765,000. Hughes was a **recluse** who never left his home. When he heard about the book, he called reporters to complain. A forensic expert used a voiceprint to confirm that the speaker was definitely Howard Hughes. The two forgers confessed to their crime and were sent to prison for **fraud**.

The Ripper

From 1975 to 1980, a killer in the UK brutally murdered 13 women. After a long investigation, the Yorkshire Ripper was arrested and sent to prison for life.

One reason it took so long to catch him was because the police received **hoax** messages from another man. Voiceprints helped to convict John Humble, the fake Yorkshire Ripper, for the false calls.

Peter Sutcliffe (the Yorkshire Ripper) was eventually arrested in 1981.

CAN YOU BELIEVE IT?

John Humble was not identified as the Yorkshire Ripper hoaxer for over 20 years. In 2005, DNA on one of the audiotape envelopes matched Humble's DNA sample, held on police records after a different crime. In 2006, John Humble was sentenced to eight years in prison for perverting justice.

1980s Crime

Some of the famous forensic cases of the 1980s used fairly ordinary science to catch extraordinary criminals. Some of these cases involved fibers and wriggling maggots!

Atlanta Killer

From 1979 to 1981, at least 29 people were strangled by a **serial killer** in Atlanta, Georgia. Most of the victims were children. One night, police investigating the murders heard a splash from a river and saw a car drive away. They stopped the driver, Wayne Williams, and questioned him. There was nothing to connect him to the murders until a body was found near where his car had been.

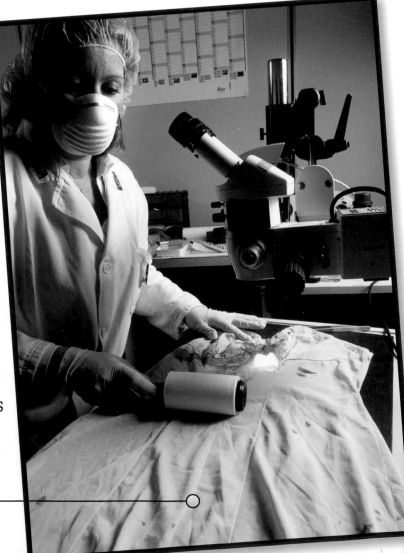

When forensic scientists examined **unique** fibers found on the murder victims, they matched items found in Williams's home. He was sent to prison for the murders in 1982.

A forensic scientist uses a roller to collect hair and fibers from a bloodstained dress.

Maggot Proof

Alton Coleman was a serial killer who terrorized Americans across six states in 1984. One of Coleman's murder victims was nine-year-old Vernita Wheat from Wisconsin. Her insect-covered body was found three weeks after she went missing.

DID YOU KNOW?

A forensic entomologist (a scientist who studies insects) can determine how long a body has been dead. Insects appear on bodies at different times. After flies, carrion beetles appear. After a year or so, the final remains likely attract only a few moths.

Coleman was a suspect, but he said he hadn't seen Vernita since taking her to a carnival weeks before. A forensic scientist examined maggots from her body. The flies' eggs had been laid only a day after the carnival. By determining the time of death, it became more likely that Coleman was the murderer. He was later convicted of his crimes and sentenced to death.

Tests on insects from a dead body can reveal exactly when the victim died.

Groundbreaking Science

One of the greatest breakthroughs in forensic science came in the 1980s with the development of DNA **profiles**. This amazing work changed crime scene science forever.

What Is It?

DNA is material found in each of your billions of body **cells**, including your blood, saliva, hair **follicles**, and skin. Everyone's DNA is different—except for some identical twins. As most of us leave a few cells behind wherever we go, evidence can often be collected from skin, blood, or hair samples found at a crime scene. Scientists can test the exact pattern (called a DNA fingerprint or profile) to compare two sets of DNA. If these are identical, chances are they are from the same person.

Forensic scientists take samples of DNA from a crime scene for further testing. DNA profiles can be compared to profiles already on a DNA database.

CASE FILE

In 1983, Lynda Mann, a 15-year-old schoolgirl, was found murdered in Leicestershire, UK. The police were unable to find her killer. Three years later, Dawn Ashworth, another 15-year-old girl, was found strangled nearby. This time, the police made an arrest because Richard Buckland, a local 17-year-old, was seen close to the murder scene. In a panic, he confessed to Dawn Ashworth's murder.

DID YOU KNOW?

Building on research by others before them, British scientist Francis Crick and American scientist James Watson discovered the structure of DNA in 1953. But it was not until 1984 that British scientist Sir Alec Jeffreys first developed a way to examine DNA profiles from body cells.

Using new DNA tests, scientists compared cells found at the murder scenes with a blood sample from Richard Buckland. They did not match. However, the DNA from both murder scenes was from the same man. He turned out to be Colin Pitchfork, who was sentenced to life imprisonment in 1988 for both murders. Richard Buckland was the first person to be cleared of a crime using DNA profiles.

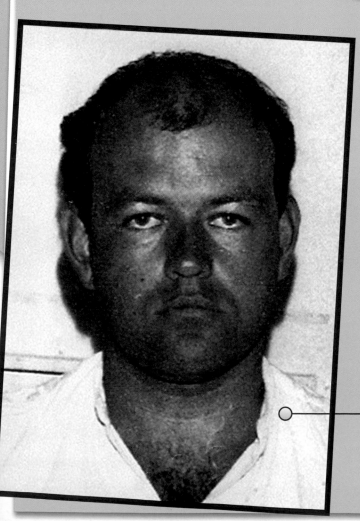

Colin Pitchfork, who murdered two 15-year-old schoolgirls in the mid-1980s, was the first person to be convicted using DNA evidence.

1990s Discovery

Modern forensic science reveals many of the secrets behind famous ancient mysteries. The discovery of a frozen mummy in 1995 amazed forensic scientists.

The Ice Maiden

In 1995, scientists in Peru saw what they thought was a backpack on the icy slopes of Mount Ampato. In fact, it was the body of a girl wrapped in cloth. She turned out to be the first frozen female mummy discovered in the Andes Mountains. A nearby volcano had melted the ice, which uncovered her body.

Called the Ice Maiden of Peru, the mummy was later discovered to be an **Inca** girl of 12–14 years of age. She had died about 500 years ago. Scientists immediately began studying Juanita—as she also became known. She became famous around the world. *Time* magazine called her one of the world's top 10 discoveries! So what was her story and how did she die?

The body of Juanita (the Ice Maiden) had been perfectly preserved in the ice.

Test Results

By using forensic tests from crime laboratories, scientists began to reveal Juanita's secrets. Pathologists carried out examinations, including DNA tests, X-rays, and the kind of **autopsy** used in murder investigations. They found:

- her bones, muscles, and teeth were in good condition,

- she showed no signs of disease and was healthy at the time of her death, and

- she was slim, ate a well-balanced diet, and had eaten vegetables but no meat a few hours before she died.

Juanita's skull was fractured above her right eye and her brain was displaced to one side. This suggested she had been hit on the side of the head with a club and most likely killed as a sacrifice to please the Incan gods.

CAN YOU BELIEVE IT?

The Ice Maiden was thought to be the best-preserved Incan mummy in the world until 1999 when three other frozen mummies were discovered in Argentina. Unlike Juanita, these well-preserved mummies (which included one called La Doncella) still had blood in their hearts and lungs.

La Doncella was discovered in 1999. She was about 15 years old when she and her two children were killed by the Incas as human sacrifices more than 500 years ago.

New Millennium

The new millennium saw exciting developments in DNA forensic science. In 2003, in the first case of its kind, DNA brought a conviction for a killer.

Crime Breakthrough

Although we all have different DNA, people from the same family have very similar DNA profiles. By comparing two people's profiles, scientists can tell if they are related to each other. If DNA found at a crime scene *almost* matches a known criminal's DNA profile, the police will want to investigate members of that criminal's family as likely suspects.

Fingerprints and DNA profiles are unique, but family members can have similar DNA samples.

CASE FILE

In 2003, Michael Little was killed when someone threw a brick from a bridge over a highway in the UK. The brick smashed through the truck's windshield and hit Michael's chest. The 53-year-old driver suffered a heart attack but managed to steer his truck to safety before he died.

Before throwing the brick, the killer had tried to steal a car by smashing its window. Forensic investigators were able to collect traces of blood from the brick, but the DNA profile did not match anyone on the UK's DNA database. The only clue was that the DNA sample belonged to a white male. Before long, the database showed a very close match to a local criminal. When the police called on one of the criminal's relatives and took a DNA sample, they found an exact match to the DNA on the brick.

Nineteen-year-old Craig Harman was found guilty of killing Michael Little. He became the first person in the world to be sent to prison because of his relative's DNA profile.

DID YOU KNOW?

The technique of finding a criminal from a family member's DNA is called **familial searching**.
"There is no doubt in my mind that without this groundbreaking technique, this crime (the killing of Michael Little) would have remained undetected."
Detective Chief Inspector Graham Hill of Surrey Police, UK.

The DNA in our bodies can be tested by forensic experts.

Famous Art

One of the most famous paintings in the world, probably worth over $70 million, made world news in 2004 when it was stolen. Forensic scientists were soon on the case.

Theft in Norway

The Scream, painted by Norwegian artist Edvard Munch in 1893, is known around the world. It made headline news when two masked men raided an Oslo art museum. The robbers grabbed the painting off the wall as one pointed a gun before running off with the valuable artwork. Visitors and staff could only watch in horror.

The thieves sped off in a black Audi, throwing out the picture frame. The police later found the abandoned getaway car. The thieves had sprayed a fire extinguisher inside the car, in the hope of destroying DNA evidence. Even so, forensic scientists were able to find useful biological **trace evidence**.

Painted in 1893, *The Scream* is Edvard Munch's most famous work.

Solving the Crime

A year after the theft, the Norwegian police had not found the painting and feared the thieves had burned it to destroy all evidence. The Norwegian government offered a reward for its safe return.

After two years of careful forensic work, the police had arrested six men. Forensic **digital evidence**, such as the study of about 60,000 phone calls, showed links to the crime. In 2006, three of the men were sent to prison and the famous painting was recovered at last.

Tiny traces of evidence can still be found inside a car even after criminals have tried to wipe it clean.

CAN YOU BELIEVE IT?

Edvard Munch (1863–1944) painted several versions of *The Scream*, some of which were targets of famous thefts. In 1994, one version, in Norway's National Gallery, was stolen but recovered months later. Four men were sentenced for that theft in 1996.

The Forensic Science Service®

Mystery Poison

A particularly puzzling murder made headline news in 2006. Forensic scientists had a difficult case to solve.

Deadly Substance

Cases of people being deliberately poisoned by deadly **radioactive** substances are very rare. It is also highly dangerous for forensic scientists and pathologists to deal with radiation crime.

Alexander Litvinenko was a former Russian spy living in London, UK. He told friends that he feared Russian agents were trying to kill him. In November 2006, Litvinenko met two Russian men in a London hotel and another in a sushi bar. A few hours later, he felt ill. After three days, he went to a hospital where doctors thought he had been poisoned. His hair fell out and within three weeks he was dead. A mysterious poison had destroyed his bone marrow and liver, eventually causing a massive heart attack.

Alexander Litvinenko was treated at a London hospital but died from radioactive poisoning.

Gathering the Evidence

Forensic scientists proved a rare radioactive substance called **polonium-210** was used to poison Litvinenko—even though it was too dangerous to carry out a full autopsy on his body.

Traces of the poison were found at places Litvinenko had recently visited, including London's Millennium Hotel and a sushi bar. Forensic scientists had a massive task testing many different places and people in order to piece together all the evidence.

Was this the deadly weapon?

DID YOU KNOW?

A forensic scientist who specializes in chemical evidence, drugs, and poisons is called a **toxicologist**. Is it a job for you? Warning—it can involve dangerous substances, maggots, victims' blood, saliva, hair, urine, and stomach contents, all in a day's work!

No Conviction

Although the police had various suspects, no one could be charged. Alexander Litvinenko's murder is likely to remain a mystery for many years. Forensic scientists worked hard to find the killers, but the secret world of international spies prevented suspects from being convicted.

Deadly radioactive substances are marked with this warning symbol.

Forensic Time Line

1901 Austrian scientist Karl Landsteiner (1868–1943) discovers human blood groups. Paul Uhlenhuth (1870–1957) discovers a way to tell human blood from animal blood.

1908 President Theodore Roosevelt establishes the Bureau of Investigation (which became the FBI in 1935).

1923 Los Angeles Police Chief August Vollmer (1876–1955) begins the first forensic laboratory. The Bureau of Forensic Ballistics is established in New York City.

1929 The ballistic work used to solve the famous St. Valentine's Day Massacre in Chicago leads to the start of the Scientific Crime Detection Laboratory (SCDL).

1932 FBI's forensic laboratory is established.

1951 The French toxicologist Henri Griffon is the first to use neutron activation analysis to detect traces of poison in hair.

| 1900 | 1910 | 1920 | 1930 | 1940 | 1950 |

1913 Victor Balthazard (1872–1950) writes that each fired bullet carries unique marks.

1910 Edmond Locard (1877–1966) opens the first forensic laboratory in Lyon, France. Thomas Jennings becomes the first U.S. citizen convicted by fingerprints.

1903 The first system for fingerprint identification in the U.S. begins in the New York State prison system.

1935 Dr. Alexander Mearns at Glasgow University uses the age of maggots on a body to determine the time of death of a victim in a murder case.

1931 John Glaister (1856–1932) publishes his landmark book on hair analysis.

John Glaister

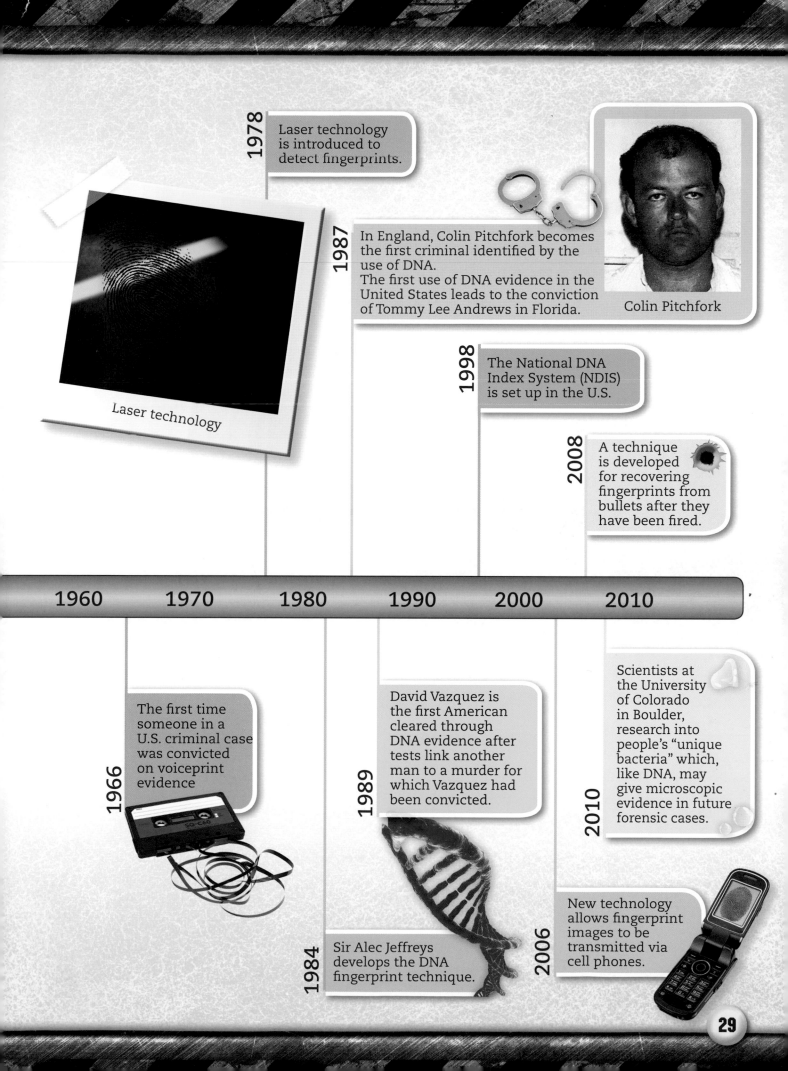

1978 Laser technology is introduced to detect fingerprints.

Laser technology

1987 In England, Colin Pitchfork becomes the first criminal identified by the use of DNA.
The first use of DNA evidence in the United States leads to the conviction of Tommy Lee Andrews in Florida.

Colin Pitchfork

1998 The National DNA Index System (NDIS) is set up in the U.S.

2008 A technique is developed for recovering fingerprints from bullets after they have been fired.

1960   1970   1980   1990   2000   2010

1966 The first time someone in a U.S. criminal case was convicted on voiceprint evidence

1989 David Vazquez is the first American cleared through DNA evidence after tests link another man to a murder for which Vazquez had been convicted.

2010 Scientists at the University of Colorado in Boulder, research into people's "unique bacteria" which, like DNA, may give microscopic evidence in future forensic cases.

1984 Sir Alec Jeffreys develops the DNA fingerprint technique.

2006 New technology allows fingerprint images to be transmitted via cell phones.

Glossary

assassin
someone who kills an important person

audio
to do with sound

autopsy
an examination of a dead body

ballistics
the science of the motion of fired objects

cells
the basic building blocks of all living things, continually being renewed

convicted
when someone is proven guilty of a crime in court

court
the place where a person is questioned and proven innocent or guilty of a crime

digital evidence
information from electronic equipment that can be used as proof

DNA
the code in each person's cells that makes everyone unique

familial searching
the use of family members' DNA to identify a closely related suspect

FBI
The U.S. Federal Bureau of Investigation

follicle
a small cavity in the skin that contains cells for growing hair

forensic
using scientific methods to investigate and establish facts in criminal courts

fraud
using dishonest methods to cheat another person of something valuable

hoax
an act intended to trick or deceive

Inca
a member of the American Indian peoples of Peru

innocent
not guilty of a crime

jury
a group of people in court who must decide whether someone is guilty or not

legal
relating to law

neutron
an atomic particle

pathology
the study of body tissue and dead bodies

polonium-210
a radioactive
element

profile
a set of results
often in the form
of a graph that
shows key
characteristics

radiation
the process of giving
off radiant energy
in the form of waves
or particles

radioactive
giving off rays of
energy or particles
that are dangerous
in high doses

ransom
something paid
or demanded for
the freedom of a
captured person

recluse
someone who lives
alone and avoids
other people

serial killer
someone who
commits a number
of murders over a
period of time

spectrograph
an instrument
for mapping and
measuring waves
of light or sound

suspect
someone thought to
be guilty of a crime

trace evidence
small amounts of
material such as
hair, pollen grains, or
soil that can be used
as proof in a crime
investigation

trajectory
the curve or path
that something
travels along

toxicologist
a scientist who
studies the
harmful effects
of chemical and
physical substances
on living things

unique
only one like it in
the world

Index

audio equipment 14
autopsy 21, 27

ballistics 12, 13, 28
blood 18, 19, 21, 23, 27, 28

Coleman, Alton 17
conviction 5, 7, 8, 15, 17, 22, 27–29
court 5

Dillinger, John 7
DNA 9, 15, 18, 19, 21–24, 29

FBI 6, 7, 8, 28
fibers 16
fingerprints 4, 5, 7, 28, 29

Galton, Francis 4
gang crime 6, 7

guns 6, 7, 12, 13, 24, 29

hair 10, 11, 18, 26–28
handwriting 8
Hughes, Howard 15

Ice Maiden 20, 21
insects 16, 17, 27, 28

Kelly, George 6, 7
Kennedy, John F. 12, 13
kidnap 6, 8, 9

Lindbergh, Charles 8, 9
Litvinenko, Alexander 26, 27

murder 5, 8, 10–13, 15, 16, 17, 19, 21, 26, 27–29

paint 5, 11

pathologist 12, 21, 26
Phillips, Robert 7
Pitchfork, Colin 19, 29

radiation 10, 26
ransom 6, 8

saliva 18, 27
skin 7, 18
spectrograph 14
suspect 5, 8, 17, 22, 27

The Scream 24, 25
toxicology 27, 28

voiceprint 14, 15, 29

Williams, Wayne 16

Yorkshire Ripper 15

Web Finder

www.fbi.gov/about-us/history
Learn all about the history of the FBI and some of its most famous cases.

www.pbs.org/wgbh/amex/lindbergh/sfeature/crime.html
Learn more about the Lindbergh kidnapping.

http://news.nationalgeographic.com/news/2007/09/photogalleries/mummy-pictures
Learn more about the frozen Inca mummies.

http://science.howstuffworks.com/biometrics3.htm
What are voiceprints and how do they help to catch criminals?

http://whyfiles.org/014forensic
Read all about cool forensics and more!